C000039392

Purple Ronnie's Star Signs

Gemini

21st May - 20th June

☆

First published 1994 by Statics (London) Ltd

This edition published 2002 by Boxtree
an imprint of Pan Macmillan Ltd
Pan Macmillan, 20 New Wharf Road, London N1 9RR
Basingstoke and Oxford
Associated companies throughout the World
www.panmacmillan.com

ISBN 0 7522 2048 9

Copyright © 1994 Purple Enterprises Ltd

The right of Giles Andreae to be identified as the
author of this work has been asserted by him in accordance
with the Copyright, Designs and Patents Act 1988.

All rights reserved. No part of this publication may be
reproduced, stored in or introduced into a retrieval system, or
transmitted, in any form, or by any means (electronic, mechanical,
photocopying, recording or otherwise) without the prior written
permission of the publisher. Any person who does any unauthorized
act in relation to this publication may be liable to criminal
prosecution and civil claims for damages.

9 8 7 6 5 4 3 2 1

A CIP catalogue record for this book is available from
the British Library

Text by Giles Andreae
Illustrations by Janet Cronin
Printed and bound in Hong Kong

☆ Introduction ☆

Star Signs are a brilliant way of finding out about someone's character. You can use them to discover anything you like including what everyone's secretest rude fantasies are.

But reading what's written in the stars can only be done by incredibly brainy people like me. After gazing for ages through my gigantic telescope and doing loads of complicated sums and

harts and stuff I have been able to
work out exactly what everyone in the
world is really like.

This book lets you know about all my
amazing discoveries. It tells you what you
look like, who your friends are, how your
love life is, what you're like at Doing It
and who you should be Doing It with.
Everything I've written in this book is
completely true. Honest.

Love from

Purple Ronnie
xox

Contents

...5 minutes later...

Gemini people make
wonderful friends
You can always break
down on their shoulder
They tell you that crying
is good now and then
And you come away
wiser and older

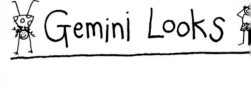

Gemini Looks

As soon as you look
at a Gemini they will
wink at you, wiggle their
bottoms and lick their lip

Gemini Men

Gemini Men are tall
and skinny when they're
young and bald and porky
when they're older.
They love wriggling around
and scratching their parts

Gemini Women

Gemini Women always look younger than they are. They have sexy legs and they like to wear groovy clothes and fancy knicker

tee hee

Gemini people never seem to grow up. They love

dashing around and
trying out new things
all the time

leap

spin

Geminis are also nervy
and fidgety...

and completely useless
t doing only one thing at
time

Gemini and Friends

Gemini people are great to have as friends because they are interested in practically everything

and this one's called Nigel
wow! how amazingly fascinating
eee eeee

Warning:-

If you are a friend of a Gemini you must be very good at listening

Geminis would be brilliant...

T.V. PRESENTERS

because:-

1. They love gossiping and spreading rumours
LIVE SHOW

2. They like travelling around all over the place

3. They love dressing up and going to fancy parties

Geminis can go through lots of lovers because they want to find the perfect match

They love chatting
people up...

...and are quite likely
to have naughty
secret affairs

☆ <u>Secret Tip</u> ☆

Geminis don't like talkin'
about deep feelings
so if you go on a
date with one you must
be careful not to
get too soppy

Gemini and Sex

Geminis like their sex life to be fun and playful and full of surprise

Sometimes Geminis get all tangled up inside their heads and what they need most is a great big warm cuddle

Geminis never
stop talking even
when they're
Doing It

The End